The Holy Spirit: The Person, The Works
Don't Live Without Him

Yolonda Troupe Smith

**The Holy Spirit: The Person, The Works
Don't Live Without Him**

Copyright © 2016 Yolonda Troupe Smith

All rights reserved. No part of this book may be used or reproduced by any means, graphic, electronic, or mechanical, including photocopying, recording, taping or by any information storage retrieval system, without the written permission of the publisher except in the case of brief quotations embodied in critical articles and reviews.

The views expressed in this work are solely those of the author and do not necessarily reflect the views of the publisher, and the publisher hereby disclaims any responsibility for them.

Entegrity Choice Publishing
PO Box 453
Powder Springs, GA 30127
info@entegritypublishing.com

Unless otherwise indicated, Scripture quotations used in this book are from the Holy Bible, King James Version.

Data quotations are from Jerry Hutchins, "Understanding the Holy Spirit."

Book Cover Designed by
Tolden Williams

ISBN: 978-0-9909397-5-7

Library of Congress Control Number: 2016938185

Printed in the United States of America

Acknowledgements

First, I would like to thank my parents, Jessie & Helen Troupe for the time that they invested in me to give me a solid foundation in Jesus, and a healthy respect for God's word.

I would like to express my gratitude to the many friends who prayed for me as I wrote this book: to all those who provided support, participated in chat sessions, read, offered comments, and assisted with editing and proofreading.

I would like to thank my son, Alphounce Williams for his input on the cover, pictures, and encouraging words. I would like to thank my son, Tolden Williams for the many hours that he worked on the cover design, pictures, and encouraging me along the process.

Thanks to The Write Person Consulting Services and Entegrity Choice Publishing for connecting the dots to make everything come together.

Above all, I want to thank my husband, Donell who supported and encouraged me from start to finish. Thanks for never having a negative response, always providing great ideas, pressing me to dig deeper in my writing, and telling me to pray for the Holy Spirit to have his way.

Finally I want to send a very special thanks to my pastor, Bishop Paul S. Morton, for his endorsement, and Co-Pastor Dr. Debra B. Morton, for writing the foreword. It is an honor to be a part of their vision and ministry as they are led by God. They are a powerful spiritual couple that epitomizes the works of the Holy Spirit. Their messages stir my inner spirit and motivate me to operate in my purpose.

God Bless you all for what you have done to make this dream a reality.

Contents

Foreword VII
Introduction IX

Part I
Holy Spirit

The Holy Spirit 13
The Holy Spirit's Purpose 17
Allow the Holy Spirit to Operate 23
    The Holy Spirit Within and Salvation 24
    My Conversion Story 24
    Effects of the Holy Spirit Within and Salvation 29
    Baptized and Filled With the Holy Spirit 30
    Results of Being Baptized and Filled With the Holy Spirit 35
    How Are Tongues Used With the Holy Spirit? 38
    Tongues Are Real: My First Experience 41

Part II
Don't Live Without Him

My Journey with the Holy Spirit 49
Moving Forward To My Destiny 89
The Holy Spirit Blueprint 95

Foreword

How refreshing it is to know that God is still filling and teaching His children about the person and power of the Holy Spirit. This brings back precious memories that changed my life and Christian walk! Having a Baptist background, I was told and believed that the power of the Holy Spirit was not for me. It was only for a certain denomination! Well, how wrong they were and how happy I was! As I allowed the Holy Spirit to live in and through me, I began to experience the Real Joy of the Lord, not just on Sundays, but everyday of my life. I then understood the song my Granny used to sing, "…and He walks with me and He talks with me and tells me I am His own!" My soul is filling up right now as I type!

In this season of chaos and fear, how powerful is it that Elder Yolonda Troupe Smith would be led by God's Spirit to teach and enlighten all who read and receive this book, how to be empowered to handle anything that comes their way! This book, "The Holy Spirit – The Person, The Works"; Don't Live Without Him", is a gift that is much needed in the Body of Christ, just as the Holy Spirit is a gift! It will enable all to walk in purpose and power, demonstrating to a lost and dark world, the ability of God to heal and set free those that are bound by darkness! It is our tool to show the POWER of God in Action!

Elder Smith, diligent and skillful in her assignment, has written a Masterpiece! Although, created by God, He has allowed her to master the subject matter through giving herself to much prayer and study as well as seeing Him work in her personal and professional life experiences!

"Thank You" Elder for relying on the Holy Spirit and pushing through your circumstances to make this happen!

Friends, please read carefully, but with anticipation, because you will never live the same again!

Dr. Debra B. Morton
Pastor, Greater St. Stephen Ministries, New Orleans, Louisiana
Co-Pastor, Changing a Generation Ministries, Atlanta, Georgia
Professional Coach

Introduction

One of the most precious things that a Christian can do is share the knowledge that God has given them to others. If everything that God has taught you can be deposited in another person they can deposit it in another person, (so forth and so on) and eventually, we can change the world.

I've been a Christian since I was nine years old and my Christian walk is still a blessing. My inspiration for writing this book stems from getting to know and appreciate the awesome gift of the Holy Spirit over many years. If you asked me back in the beginning of my journey to describe or explain the Holy Spirit, I would have responded: he's my helper, he's my comforter, he's the one that Jesus left behind for me, and I know who the Holy Spirit is.

When you read this book you will begin to understand that he is much more than that. I had to develop a personal relationship with him, and most importantly, I had to learn how to activate the power of the Holy Spirit in my life.

Why would anybody want to live any other way than our predestined ordained purpose that God has for every believer? I lived this way for many years and it was because of the lack of knowledge. Hosea 4:6 states "My people are destroyed for a lack of knowledge."

Since, what you don't know "can" hurt you, I want everyone to have a glimpse of how to get to know the Holy Spirit. I was embarrassed when I heard someone discussing the Holy Spirit. I was not knowledgeable enough on the subject to respond, so the Lord told me to go study. I had no idea this simple thought from God would change my life and later become the inspiration for a book that would change the life of other Christians.

This book is a power-packed story that concentrates on the central features of the Holy Sprit's person and work. It also chronicles my intimate experiences, encounters, and relationship with the Holy Spirit. As you read this book, you will picture my growth through my life's journey as I gave my life to Christ (*the mourner's bench experience*). You will experience highs (*miracles*) and lows (*devil worship*), twists (*divorce*) and turns (*deliverance*), becoming filled with Holy Spirit (*explosive tongue experience*) and walking in power (*taking dominion*).

I have truly learned that I cannot and will not live without Him!

Part I

Holy Spirit

Chapter One

The Holy Spirit

One of the most precious, powerful, and important weapons that a Christian has is the Holy Spirit. He is the third person that completes the trinity.

The three parts to the trinity are:

1. *God the Father*; who is the creator of all things. Everything originates and flows from Him.

2. *God the Son*; who is given to us by the Father. He paid for our sins with His blood so we can have eternal life. He is the mediator between man and God.

3. *God the Holy Spirit*; who is given to us by the Father to be our helper. By His power, believers are saved and receive help to live a life on earth which is pleasing to God.

To live a life pleasing to God, we must obey the Holy Spirit and allow him to do His job so that all Christians become all that GOD created them to be. The Holy Spirit is an awesome blessing sent to take Jesus' place when He went back to the Father.

"And I will pray the Father, and he shall give you another Comforter, that he may abide with you forever; Even the Spirit of truth; whom the world cannot receive, because it seeth him not, neither knoweth him: but ye know him; for he dwelleth with you, and shall be in you. I will not leave you comfortless: I will come to you. Yet a little while, and the world seeth me no more; but ye see me: because I live, ye shall live also."
John 14:16-19

In the scriptures, the Holy Spirit is presented as a person. He is always spoken of as "He," not "It." He is someone, not something. He speaks (1 Timothy 4:1), He teaches us (1 Cor. 2:13), He knows the thoughts of God (1 Cor. 2:11), and prays for us (Romans 8:26). He even has emotions – it is possible to grieve Him (Eph. 4:30). The Holy Spirit is therefore more than a mere force or power. He is more than something like enthusiasm. He is the very Spirit of God. He is God!

"Now the Spirit speaketh expressly, that in the latter times some shall depart from the faith, giving heed to seducing spirits, and doctrines of devils." 1 Timothy 4:1

"For what man knoweth the things of a man, save the spirit of man which is in him? Even so the things of God knoweth no man, but the Spirit of God. Which things also we speak, not in the words which man's wisdom teacheth, but which the Holy Ghost teacheth; comparing spiritual things with spiritual." 1 Corinthians 2:11,13

"Likewise the Spirit also helpeth our infirmities: for we know not what we should pray for as we ought: but the Spirit itself maketh intercession for us with groanings which cannot be uttered." Romans 8:26

"And grieve not the Holy Spirit of God, whereby ye are sealed unto the day of redemption." Ephesians 4:30

Chapter 2

The Holy Spirit's Purpose

A person is born again when they believe and receive Jesus Christ as Lord and Savior. (John 1:12-13; John 3:3-21) God resides in that person through the Holy Spirit, and the Holy Spirit acts as a believer's bible study teacher (1Cor. 3:16).

Jesus told His disciples…

"The Helper, the Holy Spirit, whom the Father will send in my name, He will teach you all things, and bring to your remembrance all that I said to you." John 14:26.

The Holy Spirit's chief functions are: to work in the life of the believer, illuminate Jesus' teaching and to glorify His person.

The Holy Spirit is the power line that connects you to Jesus, which is the power of God, and the only way to the Father. The Holy Spirit leads us into all truth and shows us how the word of God applies to our everyday lives.

The Holy Spirit convicts of sin, renews, baptizes, anoints, empowers, sanctifies, reveals things, gives discernment, gives gifts, speaks, teaches, comforts, helps, guides, protects, encourages, intercedes, and counsels his children through emotional, physical, or spiritual storms in life.

Without Him, man is unable to accomplish God's eternal purpose, or conquer and overcome the devil. He also empowers believers to perform ministerial duties that will promote spiritual growth in other believers (Rom. 12; 1Cor. 12; Eph. 4).

The Holy Spirit also performs a function for non-Christians, or non-believers, when He convicts people's hearts of God's truth concerning how sinful we are, how we need God's forgiveness, how righteous Jesus is, how he died in our place for our sins, and how God will eventually judge the world and those who do not know Him (John 16:8-11). The Holy Spirit tugs on our hearts and minds, asking us to repent and turn to God for forgiveness and a new life.

"But as many as received him, to them gave he power to become the sons of God, even to them that believe on his name: Which were born, not of blood, nor of the will of the flesh, nor of the will of man, but of God." John 1:12-13

"But the Comforter, which is the Holy Ghost, whom the Father will send in my name, he shall teach you all things, and brings all things to your remembrance, whatsoever I have said unto you." John 14:26

"Jesus answered and said unto him, Verily, verily, I say unto thee, Except a man be born again, he cannot see the kingdom of God. Nicodemus saith unto him, How can a man be born when he is old? can he enter the second time into his mother's womb, and be born? Jesus answered, Verily, verily, I say unto thee, Except a man be born of water and of the Spirit, he cannot enter into the kingdom of God. That which is born of the flesh is flesh; and that which is born of the Spirit is spirit. Marvel not that I said unto thee, Ye must be born again. The wind bloweth where it listeth, and thou hearest the sound thereof, but canst not tell whence it cometh, and whither it goeth: so is every one that is born of the Spirit. Nicodemus answered and said unto him, How can these things be? Jesus

answered and said unto him, Art thou a master of Israel, and knowest not these things? Verily, verily, I say unto thee, We speak that we do know, and testify that we have seen; and ye receive not our witness. If I have told you earthly things, and ye believe not, how shall ye believe, if I tell you of heavenly things? And no man hath ascended up to heaven, but he that came down from heaven, even the Son of man which is in heaven. And as Moses lifted up the serpent in the wilderness, even so must the Son of man be lifted up: That whosoever believeth in him should not perish, but have eternal life. For God so loved the world, that he gave his only begotten Son, that whosoever believeth in him should not perish, but have everlasting life. For God sent not his Son into the world to condemn the world; but that the world through him might be saved. He that believeth on him is not condemned: but he that believeth not is condemned already, because he hath not believed in the name of the only begotten Son of God. And this is the condemnation, that light is come into the world, and men loved darkness rather than light, because their deeds were evil. For every one that doeth evil hateth the light, neither cometh to the light, lest his deeds should be reproved. But he that doeth truth cometh to the light, that his deeds may be made manifest, that they are wrought in God. John 3:3-21

"But as it is written, Eye hath not seen, nor ear heard, neither have entered into the heart of man, the things which God hath prepared for them that love him. But God hath revealed them unto us by his Spirit: for the Spirit searcheth all things, yea, the deep things of God. For what man knoweth the things of a man, save the spirit of man which is in him? Even so the things of God knoweth no man, but the Spirit of God. Now we have received, not the spirit of the world, but the spirit which is of God; that we might know the things that are freely given to us

of God. Which things also we speak, not in the words which man's wisdom teacheth, but which the Holy Ghost teacheth; comparing spiritual things with spiritual. But the natural man receiveth not the things of the Spirit of God: for they are foolishness unto him: neither can he know them, because they are spiritually discerned." I Corinthians 2:9-14

"Know ye not that ye are the temple of God, and that the Spirit of God dwelleth in you?" I Corinthians 3:16

"How be it when he, the Spirit of truth, is come, he will guide you into all truth: for he shall not speak of himself; but whatsoever he shall hear, that shall he speak: and he will shew you things to come." John 16:13

"And when he is come, he will reprove the world of sin, and of righteousness, and of judgement: Of sin, because they believe not on me; Of righteousness, because I go to my Father, and ye see me no more; Of judgement, because the prince of this world is judged. John 16:8-11

Yolonda Troupe Smith

Chapter 3

Allow the Holy Spirit to Operate

The Holy Spirit Within and Salvation

The Holy Spirit convicts the sinner and draws him to the Lord. The human body is the temple that the Holy Spirit must be invited in to dwell. The moment we believe in Jesus as our Savior (which is salvation, Romans 10:9), the Holy Spirit dwells in us permanently.

Salvation is our spiritual conversion experience and is the beginning of the Christian walk of discipleship, or life. An invisible receipt of the Holy Spirit occurs at conversion and joins us with other believers into the body of Christ.

Becoming a child of God is a spiritual birth. When we are first born, we are born of our natural parents. When we are born "again," we are born of God.

How does one become born again? *"Confess with thy mouth the LORD Jesus Christ, and believe in your heart that God raised him from the dead, and thou shalt be saved." Romans 10:9*

After we do this we are saved, born again, and converted. We become new creations in Christ.

My Conversion Story

As long as I can remember, I attended church every Sunday and at least one other day of the week. Sunday school was the time that all of my friends gathered in a classroom and we discussed the bible scriptures year after year. The books we used for our age were good and the stories were enjoyable. Attending Sunday School was my foundation. When I reached the age of nine, I asked my parents for guidance and permission to get saved. I knew I had to answer a few questions from the pastor to show that I was ready to begin the process.

For example:

1. Do you believe that Jesus was God's son?

2. Do you believe that Jesus was crucified, died, and was buried, and rose again with all power in His hands?

3. Do you believe that God's son gave His life to give you the right to eternal life?

I believed that all three of these questions were true. God was real and He loved me. I did not realize there was a process to become saved.

First, I had to take a week of my life to do the following:

1. Do not play, only sit in a chair and think about God's love for me, Jesus dying for me, and becoming a part of God's family. I also had to pray, ask God to forgive me of my sins, ask Him to show me my ways that did not please Him and help me to live right.

2. No television, just meditate and talk to God all week.

3. Go to church each night during the week and sit on the first bench in the church (the Mourner's Bench). The bench was near the pulpit stand and it was full of young girls and boys who desired forgiveness

from sin and expected new life from Christ after conversion. We listened to the sermon each night that drew us closer to the Lord. We were taught that we were sinners but because of Jesus, we can be saved by grace.

At the end of each night, the preacher closed the sermon and pleaded with us (unsaved young people) to come to the altar. He pleaded for us to rise up before the congregation and confess that we were sinners saved by grace.

The last night of the week had arrived; I can remember it as if it was yesterday. Five nights had passed and each night no one rose up to come to Christ. I guess, no one wanted to be the first to step out, or the enemy was working to keep us all on the bench with no one being saved. All of a sudden, something came over me! I was overtaken with tears as something happened--God touched me. It was unbelievable! I had prayed all week, given up my playtime, heard the word all week, and finally Saturday night, I got a touch from God. I can still see the picture in my mind.

That little church was filled with the power of God. We all moved off that bench that night and went up a little higher in our Christian walk. We accepted Christ as our personal savior and we were now Christians. We had become a new creature. We were more aware of right and wrong and heaven and hell. We had crossed over to the Lord's side, we were saved, we were scheduled for the baptism ceremony, and ready to grow physically and spiritually.

There is a great joy in the salvation phase of our Christian walk, because we join the royal family of God. We symbolize joining God's family as Christians through water baptism. The act of baptism demonstrates to the world that we have decided to put our trust in Jesus Christ and to obey his commands in our daily lives.

Going under the water symbolizes the new believer is dying to the "old person" inside, and when lifted from the water, the act represents becoming a new creature in Christ. We are coming out of the darkness and into the marvelous light of the gospel (Romans 6:1-11).

Baptism represents Christ's death, burial, and resurrection and is a requirement within the Great Commandment. He commanded us to *"Go ye therefore, and teach all nations, baptizing them in the name of the Father and of the Son, and of the Holy Ghost." Matthew 28:19*

"That if thou shalt confess with thy mouth the LORD Jesus, and shalt believe in thine heart that God hath raised him from the dead, thou shalt be saved." Romans 10:9

"What shall we say then? Shall we continue in sin, that grace may abound? God forbid. How shall we, that are dead to sin, live any longer therein? Know ye not, that so many of us as were baptized into Jesus Christ were baptized into his death? Therefore we are buried with him by baptism into death: that like as Christ was raised up from the dead by the glory of the Father, even so we also should walk in newness of life. For if we have been planted together in the likeness of his death, we shall be also in the likeness of his resurrection: Knowing this, that our old man is crucified with him, that the body of sin might be destroyed, that henceforth we should not serve sin. For he

that is dead is freed from sin. Now if we be dead with Christ, we believe that we shall also live with him: Knowing that Christ being raised from the dead dieth no more; death hath no more dominion over him. For in that he died, he died unto sin once: but in that he liveth, he liveth unto God. Likewise reckon ye also yourselves to be dead indeed unto sin, but alive unto God through Jesus Christ our Lord." Romans 6:1-11

"For every one that useth milk is unskilful in the word of righteousness: for he is a babe." Hebrews 5:13

"And I, brethren, could not speak unto you as unto spiritual, but as unto carnal, even as unto babes in Christ." 1 Corinthians 3:1

"As newborn babes, desire the sincere milk of the word that ye may grow thereby." 1 Peter 2:2

"The thief cometh not, but for to steal, and to kill and to destroy: I am come that they might have life, and that they might have it more abundantly." John 10:10

"Nay, in all these things we are more than conquerors through him that loved us." Romans 8:37

"This only would I learn of you, Received ye the Spirit by the works of the law, or by the hearing of faith?" Galatians 3:2

Effects of the Holy Spirit Within and Salvation

The Holy Spirit's purpose begins once a believer confesses that Jesus is Lord and receives the free gift of salvation. He takes us through the stages of a babe in Christ, to a mature Christian, and finally on to life everlasting.

As the believer's relationship continues to mature in Christ, their life will begin to bear the fruits of the Spirit. God loves us so much that He wants to share His character with us. When we allow the Holy Spirit to live in us, we start to grow and become more like God.

We should draw our strength and character from our roots, the Holy Spirit, just like a tree draws strength from its roots. As a tree strengthens and grows, it produces the fruit for that tree. As a believer strengthens and grows in the knowledge of God, over time the fruits of the Spirit are also produced.

The fruits of the Spirit are listed in Galatians 5: 22-23, *"But the fruit of the Spirit is love, joy, peace, longsuffering, gentleness, goodness, faith, Meekness, temperance: against there is no law."* "Wilmington's Guide to the Bible" explains the fruits of the Spirit as:

- Love – divine concern for others.
- Joy – inward peace and sufficiency
- Peace – a confidence and quietness of the soul
- Longsuffering – patience, endurance without quitting
- Gentleness – kindness
- Goodness – love in action
- Faith – dependability

- Meekness – subdued strength
- Temperance – self-control

Baptized and Filled With the Holy Spirit

Being saved with the Holy Spirit dwelling inside is great – but there is no power. In order to live a totally victorious life, we must operate in the power of the Holy Spirit.

The enemy (satan) is working harder than ever to do his job as stated in John 10:10.

He is trying to destroy as many believers as he can and he wants to take your power--or convince you that you have no power!

During my early twenties, I made another great step in my life. One night, while attending a non-denominational church, I stepped forward during the weekly bible study to be baptized with or filled with the Holy Spirit.

The pastor always preached a great sermon and that night was no different. He asked if anyone wanted the Holy Spirit to rule and reign over their life. He also stated a person could not live a life of victory without the Holy Spirit. A flame ignited inside me to desire the Holy Spirit and to live for Jesus. I rose up and stepped forward.

Someone volunteered to pray with me. She walked with me as I moved back and forth throughout the church. I wanted to speak in tongues. I prayed and walked and walked and prayed, but I never experienced speaking in tongues that night. I was so disappointed. I did my part to invite the Holy Spirit to take control of my life, and although I believed that I was filled or baptized with the Holy Spirit, there was no outward sign.

I was saved, filled with the Holy Spirit, and I had all that I needed to win the Christian race until my physical death.

Sometimes the period between salvation and physical death can be long and sometimes shorter. We cannot combat demonic spirits that attack us, or live a victorious life on our own strength. A Christian needs 'more of God' to experience victorious life and God wants us to have everything we need to be able to win (Romans 8:37).

The promise of the baptism with the Holy Spirit is for every believer, but the individual must ask, yield, and receive (Joel 2:28-29). It is one thing to be saved and quite another thing to be baptized with the Holy Spirit.

When believers allow the Holy Spirit to accomplish His purpose in them they will eventually become baptized with the Holy Spirit. After being empowered by the Holy Spirit, He will do a great work in their lives. All believers experience the Holy Spirit within during the moment they believe, and can be baptized with the Holy Spirit, either then or later. I personally believe that it is possible for a person to be saved and yet, not receive the baptism of the Holy Spirit; missing the blessing.

John predicted that Jesus would baptize with the Holy Spirit (Luke 3:16; John 1:33), he was clearly speaking to more than the apostles. *"John answered, saying unto them all, I indeed baptize you with water… he shall baptize you with the Holy Ghost and with fire:" Luke 3:16*

The Holy Spirit produces God's character in the believer's life in a way we cannot do on our own. The Holy Spirit builds us with love, joy, peace, patience, kindness, goodness, faithfulness, gentleness and self-control (Galatians 5:22-23). God asks us to rely on Him to produce these qualities in our lives. Thus, believers are told to walk in the Spirit and not according to the flesh (Galatians 5:25).

As the believer's relationship continues to mature in Christ, their life will bear the fruits of the spirit and they will operate in their spiritual gifts. Without God's power, it is impossible for the believer to walk in the spirit. We receive this power after the Holy Spirit has come upon us, or we are baptized with the Holy Spirit (Acts 1:8). This process is what the believer needs in order to have a victorious life but the baptism is not just for one time!

For example, when we fill our car with gas we can drive to a destination and we have a ½ tank. As we continue to drive to another destination we have ¼ tank. If we continue to drive and never go back to the gas station to refill, we will eventually run out of gas. When this car becomes empty, it is no longer able to operate in its purpose.

We can compare this to a Holy Spirit filled believer. Once we are filled, we begin to enjoy victory in Jesus. If we begin to live from day to day, never fasting, never praying, never seeking God, and never using our prayer language, we become dry and empty.

If we let ourselves become empty, then old demons try to come back home and bring friends (Mathew 12:43-45), and we will not be empowered to defeat them.

So, like the car we must refill. We must pray, seek, fast, study, and more, if we want to have total victory over all things. To live victoriously we need Jesus, and the Holy Spirit. With the Holy Spirit, we can endure things that we never could have done on our own.

If it wasn't for the Holy Spirit we would have lost our mind, committed a crime, died, committed suicide and a host of other things. The Holy Spirit really renews, anoints, empowers, sanctifies, reveals things, gives discernment, gives gifts, speaks, teaches, comforts, helps, guides, protects, encourages, intercedes, and counsels his children through emotional, physical, and spiritual storms in life.

In Matthew 3:16, Jesus was filled with the Holy Spirit. If Jesus had to be filled then you know that we have to be filled. As we stay empowered with the filling of the Holy Spirit our life takes a different direction. As we are filled, we overflow and spread to others for witnessing and for ministry.

"And it shall come to pass afterward, that I will pour out my spirit upon all flesh; and your sons and your daughters shall prophesy, your old men shall dream dreams, your young men shall see visions: And also upon the servants and upon the handmaids in those days will I pour out my spirit."
Joel 2:28-29

"John answered, saying unto them all, I indeed baptize you with water, the same said unto me, Upon whom thou shalt see the Spirit descending, and remaining on him, the same is he which baptized with the Holy Ghost." Luke 3:16

"And I knew him not: but he that sent me to baptize with water, the same said unto me, Upon whom thou shalt see the Spirit descending, and remaining on him, the same is he which baptizeth with the Holy Ghost." John 1:33

"But the fruit of the Spirit is love, joy, peace, longsuffering, gentleness, goodness, faith, Meekness, temperance: against such there is no law. And they that are Christ's have crucified the flesh with the affections and lusts. If we live in the Spirit, let us also walk in the Spirit." Galatians 5:22-25

"But ye shall receive power, after the Holy Ghost is come upon you: and ye shall be witnesses unto me both in Jerusalem, and in Judea, and in Samaria, and unto the uttermost part of the earth." Acts 1:8

When the unclean spirit is gone out of a man, he walketh through dry places, seeking rest, and findeth none. Then he saith, I will return into my house from whence I came out; and when he is come, he findeth it empty, swept, and garnished. Then goeth he, and taketh with himself seven other spirits more wicked than himself, and they enter in and dwell there: and the last state of that man is worse than the first. Even so shall it be also unto this wicked generation." Matthew 12:43-45

"And Jesus, when he was baptized, went up straightway out of the water: and, lo, the heavens were opened unto him, and he saw the Spirit of God descending like a dove, and lighting upon him." Matthew 3:16

Results of Being Baptized and Filled With the Holy Spirit

The Holy Spirit gives spiritual gifts to believers when they accept the Lord Jesus Christ as Savior. These gifts are to glorify the Father, and edify the believers and the Church. The service of the believer is to be in proportion to the gift that he possesses. The list of spiritual gifts found in Ephesians 4:7-13, Romans 12:3-8, and 1Corinthians 13 includes wisdom, knowledge, faith, healing, miracles, prophecy, discerning of spirits, speaking in tongues, and interpretation of tongues.

Believers only operate in these gifts after baptism with the Holy Spirit.

i. *Wisdom* – God given ability to resolve a situation. *1 Corinthians 12:7-11*
ii. *Knowledge* – supernaturally making something understood that you did not know. *1 Corinthians 12:7-11*
iii. *Faith* – supernatural firm belief in God's ability. *1 Corinthians 12:7-11*
iv. *Gifts of Healing* – supernatural deliverance from disease and infirmities *1 Corinthians 12:7-11*
v. *Working of miracles* – supernatural acts of God done through the believer. *1 Corinthians 12:7-11*
vi. *Prophecy* – is a supernatural word from God given to his people through a person. *1 Corinthians 12:7-11*
vii. *Discernment of Spirits* – supernatural ability from God to know if a spirit was from God, from satan, or a man. *1 Corinthians 12:7-11*

viii.   *Apostleship* – given supernatural authority to govern and create disciples, a church starter or planter. *1 Corinthians 12:28, Ephesians 4:11*

ix.   *Gift of Giving* – the supernatural ability to gather and share money and goods to others. *Romans 12:8*

x.   *Gift of Mercy* – supernatural ability to aid those in need. *Romans 12:8*

xi.   *Gift of Exhortation* – the supernatural ability to uplift others. *Romans 12:8*

xii.   *Gift of Ministering* – the supernatural ability to give help in spiritual and physical matters. *Romans 12:7, 1 Corinthians 12:28*

xiii.   *Gift of Administration* – the supernatural ability to direct, and organize others. *Romans 12:8, 1 Corinthians 12:28*

xiv.   *Gift of Teaching* – the supernatural ability to make the word of God easier to understand. *Romans 12:7, 1 Corinthians 12:28*

xv.   *Gift of Evangelism* – the supernatural ability to lead others to Christ. *Ephesians 4:11*

xvi.   *Tongues* – supernatural ability to speak in a language unknown to the speaker. *1 Corinthians 12:7-11, 14:21*

"And God hath set some in the church, first apostles, secondarily prophets, thirdly teachers after that miracles, then gifts of healings, helps, governments, diversities of tongues." 1 Corinthians 12:28

"But unto every one of us is given grace according to the measure of the gift of Christ. Wherefore he saith, When he ascended up on high, he led captivity captive, and gave gifts unto men. (Now that he ascended, what is it but that

he also descended first into the lower parts of the earth? He that descended is the same also that ascended up far above all heavens, that he might fill all things.) And he gave some, apostles; and some, prophets; and some, evangelists; and some, pastors and teachers; For the perfecting of the saints, for the work of the ministry, for the edifying of the body of Christ: Till we all come in the unity of the faith, and of the knowledge of the Son of God, unto a perfect man, unto the measure of the stature of the fullness of Christ:" Ephesians 4:7-13

"For I say, through the grace given unto me, to every man that is among you, not to think of himself more highly than he ought to think; but to think soberly, according as God hath dealt to every man the measure of faith. For as we have many members in one body, and all members have not the same office: So we, being many, are one body in Christ, and every one members one of another. Having then gifts differing according to the grace that is given to us, whether prophecy, let us prophesy according to the proportion of faith; Or ministry, let us wait on our ministering: or he that teacheth, on teaching; Or he that exhorteth, on exhortation: he that giveth, let him do it with simplicity; he that ruleth, with diligence; he that sheweth mercy, with cheerfulness." Romans 12:3-8

"But the manifestation of the Spirit is given to every man to profit withal. For to one is given by the Spirit of the word of wisdom; to another the word of knowledge by the same Sprit; To another faith by the same Spirit; to another the gifts of healing by the same Spirit; To anther the working of miracles; to another prophecy; to another discerning of spirits; to another divers kinds of tongues; to another the interpretation of tongues: But all these worketh that one and the self-same

Spirit, dividing to every man severally as he will." 1 Corinthians 12:7-11

"In the law it is written, with men of other tongues and other lips will I speak unto this people and yet for all that will they not hear me, saith the Lord." 1 Corinthians 14:21

"And be not drunk with wine, wherein is excess; but be filled with the Spirit; Speaking to yourselves in psalms and hymns and spiritual songs, singing and making melody in your heart to the Lord." Ephesians 5:18,19

How Are Tongues Used With the Holy Spirit?

Four Purposes of Tongues

1. *To Control The Whole Body*

When you submit your tongue to the Holy Spirit and allow him to speak an unlearned language through you, this shows complete surrendering.

"But the tongue can no man tame; it is an unruly evil, full of deadly poison." James 3:8

2. *For A Sign*

The multitude at Pentecost came to hear the noise abroad about the tongues, and they got the preaching of the gospel. The disciples were filled with the Holy Spirit and spoke in other tongues unknown to them, but known to people there. The Holy Spirit has used the mouth of man to speak in the language of the people so God can speak to men.

"And they were all filled with the Holy Ghost, and began to speak with other tongues, as the Spirit gave them utterance." Acts 2:4

"Wherefore tongues are for a sign, not to them that believe, but to them that believe not: but prophesying serveth not for them that believe not, but for them which believe." II Corinthians 14:22

3. To Speak To God

The Holy Spirit uses the mouth of man, letting the Spirit rule the individual. This example of tongues as a gift of the Holy Spirit is sometimes referred to as an individual's prayer language or used to edify the individual. He is awesome, the most-high God and what He does can't be wrong but is in order. As long as we follow His instructions, we are in order.

"For he that speaketh in an unknown tongue speaketh not unto men, but unto God: for no man understandeth him; howbeit in the sprit he speaketh mysteries" I Corinthians 14-2

"I thank my God, I speak with tongues more that ye all." I Corinthians 14:18

4. For Edification

We are God's children and we are surrounded by sin, sinners, temptation, trials, and the fiery darts of the devil, all working to pull us down. If we don't follow God's instruction on how to keep our temples in order, the human body and mind will be destroyed.

"He that speaketh in an unknown tongue edifieth himself; but he that prophesieth edifieth the church." I Corinthians 14:4

According to Jerry Hutchins in his book "Understanding the Holy Spirit," there are three types of tongues:

1. *The speaker doesn't understand the language but the hearer understands.* God is speaking to his people. In Acts 2:1-4,8,11, people were from all over the country and in order for the message to get to everyone, the gift of tongues allowed every man to hear in his own language; supernatural act of God to draw unbelievers to him.

2. *The speaker nor the hearer does not understand the language, but God is speaking to the people so he sends someone to interpret.* It can be the speaker or someone else. This is being done in public worship and this must be done in order. The Holy Spirit is delivering a message to the church through the speaker. The interpretation of the message must be done so that people won't hear the unknown language and think that you are insane. 1Corinthians 14:5,6,27,28, supernatural act of God to draw unbelievers to him.

3. *The speaker does not understand the language but he is talking to God and God understands what is being said.* This is the Holy Spirit directing the praying. This is only done in private worship. This worship experience is sometimes called prayer language, or praying in the spirit. This is how the believers build themselves up to live a life to please God. 1 Corinthians 14:2,4, Ephesians 6:18 Jude 1:20.

This is a supernatural act of God given to the believer to see.

Every believer must utilize the wonderful blessing that Jesus left for us. The Holy Spirit is just what we need to be able to live a life pleasing to GOD. If we follow His lead, we will bear fruits of the spirit and operate in our spiritual gifts. What a victorious life! When the people of God allow the Trinity to work completely for us, we will have the key to victorious living on earth.

Tongues Are Real: My First Experience

As I continued to travel on this Christian journey God customized some experiences that drove me to grow spiritually. I am not at liberty to tell all parts of the story but I will share the version that the Holy Spirit cleared.

During my twenties or thirties God gave me the characteristics of a spiritual magnet. Young people loved to chat with me about music, relationships, careers, and how to handle life's challenges. I crossed paths with a young person that shared his story about a past experience with devil worship activity. Oh my God, why did I have to cross his path? I did not want to fellowship with him.

My definition of fellowship, which I picked up from one of my past pastors, was two fellows in a ship working on the same goal. We had nothing in common. Or, at least, I did not think that we had anything in common. The chats with him were very scary. He mentioned when his family moved to a new city he began to hang out with neighbors that practiced beliefs I believed were from the pits of hell. Their practices, as he explained, included skinning infants, drinking blood and many ungodly events that had me shaking in my shoes as I listened to him tell the stories. This young man even had a collection of satanic books in his possession he wanted to share with me. I remember telling him that he needed to go to God and stop dealing with the devil. I told him God had all power in His hands and he needed to join the winning side.

We chatted often and his stories always left me concerned. I didn't know why God had me to listen to him or what I should say. One day he told me, "I enjoy every time that I chat with you. You think you're slick because you talk about a thousand things but before you end, you always put a little Jesus in it."

Sometime later, he shared with me that he actually believed that God was not a God of love because He took something away from him that he loved, and that made him view God differently.

I listened and talked to God as he talked and shared with me. He explained that when he was approached by a cult he entered with ease because he was so angry with God. I had not in my whole life up to that point, ever spoken with anyone that praised satan and despised God. I was not equipped for this type of talk at the time. I was not a minister yet, and I did not know the proper scriptures to recite to him. I did know *1 John 4:4 – "Ye are of God, little children, and have overcome them: because greater is he that is in you, than he that is in the world."* As I continued to listen, fearful emotions overtook me but I remembered 2 Timothy

1:7 (NKJV), *"For God has not given us a spirit of fear, but of power and of love and of a sound mind."*

All I wanted to do was show him that I was not afraid of him, even though I was terrified. I could not tell him that God had all power in His hands and then let the young person think that God did not have my back. I sat up in my seat and presented myself as a warrior for the king, even though I knew that I was not mentality armed for this battle. I did not know if he was telling the truth or not, but I had become more concerned about him spending eternity in hell. I went home one afternoon, got on my knees and began to pray for him until I cried and it seemed as if the tears would never end. *"For he that speaketh in an unknown tongue speaketh not unto men, but unto God: for no man understandeth him; howbeit in the sprit he speaketh mysteries." I Corinthians 14-2*

Tears poured down my face. I cried and prayed until my tongue became loose, and moved fast. I didn't know what I was saying, but I knew that the Holy Spirit had consumed me and I was in prayer for him. I began to remember when I read about this in the bible and from observation during my time in church. I spoke in tongues as the spirit gave me utterance (Acts 2:4). This act was what I waited for in that interdenominational church the night that I came forth to be filled with the Holy Spirit. Can you believe that God has so much love for his creation that He would direct me to pray for someone else that did not care for Him at all? I cried out to God on behalf of someone else with problems, and God heard my cry. God used me to pray for someone else and that prayer changed things.

After this powerful outpouring of the Spirit on me and through me, whenever we met after that, I was a mouthpiece for God and there was no fear in me. I became an overcomer in this situation by the blood of the lamb. As I allowed the Holy Spirit to use me to work on his business, God took care of my business. I grew spiritually! This trial, this assignment of listening to a demonic story, shaped a young person's life and shifted me to the next level. I had been saved, filled with the Holy Spirit, and I finally had the evidence of speaking in tongues. It felt good to be used by God to change things for someone else. The young man was brought out of the darkness into the marvelous light. I praise God for the Holy Spirit and the use of tongues.

"And when the day of Pentecost was fully come, they were all with one accord in one place. And suddenly there came a sound from heaven as of a rushing mighty wind, and it filled all the house where they were sitting. And there appeared unto them cloven tongues like as of fire, and it sat upon each of them. And they were all filled with the Holy Ghost, and began to speak with other tongues, as the Spirit gave them utterance. Acts 2:1-4

"And how hear we every man in our own tongue, wherein we were born?" Acts 2:8

"Cretes and Arabians, we do hear them speak in our tongues the wonderful works of God." Acts 2:11

"For he that speaketh in an unknown tongue speaketh not unto men, but unto God: for no man understandeth him; howbeit in the spirit he speaketh mysteries. But he that prophesieth speaketh unto men to edification, and exhortation, and comfort. He that speaketh in an unknown tongue edifieth

himself; but he that prophesieth edifieth the church. I would that ye all spake with tongues but rather that ye prophesied: for greater is he that prophesieth than he that speaketh with tongues except he interpret, that the church may receive edifying. Now, brethren, if I come unto you speaking with tongues, what shall I profit you, except I shall speak to you either by revelation, or by knowledge, or by prophesying, or by doctrine?" 1 Corinthians 14:2-6

"If any man speaks in an unknown tongue, let it be by two, or at the most by three, and that by course; and let one interpret. But if there be no interpreter, let him keep silence in the church; and let him speak to himself, and to God" 1 Corinthians 14:27-28

"Praying always with all prayer and supplication in the Spirit, and watching thereunto with all perseverance and supplication for all saints." Ephesians 6:18

"But ye, beloved, building up yourselves on your most holy faith, praying in the Holy Ghost." Jude 1:20

Part II

Don't Live Without Him

Chapter 4

My Journey with the Holy Spirit

Elementary Years

At the young age of nine, I found myself asking my parents if I could get on the "*mourners bench.*" This term was used in the Baptist church for the candidates that decided to become a believer in the Christian Faith.

During a week of night services, a minister would conduct a revival and teach the Word of God. The candidates would spend all of their free time meditating and praying on their decision to follow Christ. I was so excited to join the Christian family that I did not wait for the revival at my church; I went to another church in our community with a friend. I was ready. By the end of the week, I came forward, confessed that Jesus was Lord, and crossed over on the Lord's side. I was saved!

I had begun the process from a being a babe in Christ to that of a mature Christian. Most of my life from elementary school age until now I have gone to church on Sunday. I remember when my family attended a Baptist church three Sundays a month and a Methodist church once a month. My Dad was a member of the Methodist faith, and we went to his church once a month. During this time, I learned the bible stories and examples of how Christians should conduct themselves but I never gained clarity or was taught on the subject of the Holy Spirit.

I knew that Acts 2 outlined the day of Pentecost and that the Holy Spirit appeared on the people like tongues of fire. They spoke in tongues, languages unknown to themselves, but others in the room understood. Exciting as this event may have been, that was all of the knowledge that I knew concerning the Holy Spirit in my Baptist and Methodist upbringing.

High School Years

To illustrate the importance of younger people having a Holy Spirit experience, let me relate to you a situation during my high school years.

We had a well sought-after church choir. We received invitations to sing all over our hometown. Once, we were invited to a Church of God in Christ choir day, and during the service people began to speak in tongues. We were absolutely speechless for a few minutes but being so young, our minds quickly went back to choir day. Because I did not understand what was going on, I dismissed the experience, and I didn't think about the Holy Spirit, the prayer language or the Pentecost experience again until my college days. Had someone taught me about the Holy Spirit at that point, I don't think I would have been able to understand; I had no foundation.

College Years

Things continued to change during my sophomore year in college, and I began attending another Church of God in Christ service on a sporadic basis. The pastor at that church was a gifted teacher and preacher. He had the ability to bring a message that literally lifted the words of the Bible off the pages, and made them come to life. I always left the service knowing how to apply the message to my everyday life. The Word of God had never touched me that way before.

Pretty soon, I was hooked and attended that church regularly until I graduated and obtained my Bachelor's Degree. God finally had my total attention, because I understood how to apply His word to my situation and preaching made sense!

Graduate School

When I attended graduate school, I sang in several choirs and groups, allowing me to meet lots of people from different religious denominational backgrounds. I began receiving invitations to different churches.

The churches that really got my attention, i.e. "hooked me," were the Methodist services and the "Church of God in Christ" services. Although the services were primarily different in style and procedure, both had wonderful messages, and I grew mightily in the knowledge of the Lord. God was setting me up for the destiny that he had for me and I had no clue. *God was always behind the scenes shaping my destiny.*

One of the most profound changes in my life happened while I was in graduate school. A lady, I will call her Ms. Jones, came into the dormitory on my college campus and talked about the love of Jesus. Her eyes looked so different than any other person that I had seen in my life. Her eyes captivated you and drew you to her. She was so calm and full of *love,* and her eyes shone brightest when she spoke about Jesus. So, when she came on our dormitory floor and invited me to attend bible study once a week, I didn't think twice about going-- I went. She encouraged us to learn scripture. She sewed pouches from fabric to keep the scripture cards, and she made the cards that contained some of her favorite scriptures. I felt that everything was done with love. I still actually have my pouch and cards that she made for me back in 1985 (30-years ago).

I continue to cherish this pouch for what it represents, her love for the LORD, and my love of her loving and caring spirit. Although the Church of God in Christ ignited the flame that started the fire for my journey, Mrs. Jones was used by the LORD to keep my flame burning by encouraging me to learn scriptures. I have often wondered if she is still alive and if so, where she lives. I would love to say "thank you" and give her a hug for what she deposited in me. *God was always behind the scenes shaping my destiny.*

Another one of my most memorable experiences during my final year of graduate school was when I began to attend a non-denominational church service during weeknights. The word was so enlightening, moving, and powerful, that it drew me closer, like a moth to a flame. When I began to attend church services on Sunday, in addition to the mid-week service, I knew something was going on with me, something was very different. After a few months, Sunday service was no longer enough for me, because my craving for the Word of God had surpassed the pull of anything the world had to offer. I lost my desire to attend the college parties. No one persuaded me. I had changed.

The *Word of God* was breathing, moving, and coming to life right before my very eyes. The weekly bible studies at the church were infused with fuel, igniting my heart, and the teaching burned within me long after I left the service. I was literally on-fire and that had me excited to hear more of the Word. I started chasing after the Word, seeking the Word, and embracing the Word. Every time that the Word was being taught; I wanted to have my face in the place.

Adulthood

After I finished all of my graduate classes, I taught Computer Science at a small community college. It was during that time, I began to attend a weekly "Lunch & Learn" bible study at the college. We brought our lunch and learned more about God. I was finally ready to go all-in for the Lord and everything He had to offer.

One night, at the nondenominational church that I was attending, I stepped forward during the weekly bible study to be baptized with or filled with The Holy Spirit.

I learned information about the Holy Spirit during my graduate school time, and I did not want to miss any part that God had for me. My mind was renewed and I loved every minute of it. I was so excited and I wanted to come to church as many times as there was a service.

While in graduate school, I was free to continue to attend different denominational services, but whenever I returned home to visit my parents, I was expected to attend my home church. I loved what I learned when I attended church in other locations but at the same time I wanted to honor my parents and my heritage. By this time, I really wanted more of the Holy Spirit. Although I chose to attend my regular church on Sunday, I attended the non-denominational church during the week. I had the best of both worlds and loved it. I began to read and study the Word more and the Lord began to transform me by the renewing of my mind. Many of my bad habits, incomplete goals, and misplaced desires changed. *God was always behind the scenes shaping my destiny.*

During my mid-twenties, I was saved, filled with the Holy Spirit, and aware of the unlimited power of God. This was a good place to finally reach in my life, but I was still so far from the abundant life that God has predestined and ordained for me.

Getting to Know the Holy Spirit

So, my journey begins as a Holy Spirit filled child of the king. I began to pray to God about the things going on in my life but I found that I had a problem; I still did not fully trust Him. If His answer was too much for me to do on my own, or against my will, I would go in the direction away from God's instructions.

I know that was crazy with my newly discovered gift of the Holy Spirit, but I did choose my way sometime. I did not know to call on the Holy Spirit to help me and strengthen me to obey God's will. I did not know He had a specific purpose in my life, and I certainly did not know how to activate the Holy Spirit in my daily walk. I still lived my life following God's instruction as handed down by my mother, father, and older friends. My prayer time was usually in times of trouble and at night before bed with the old memorized prayer from my younger years. *"Now I lay me down to sleep. I pray the Lord my soul to keep. If I should die before I wake, I pray the Lord my soul to take. Amen*

I was an adult, still praying the Kid's Prayer; how sad. I also added the Lord's Prayer but I am still praying memorized prayers. I did not have a clue of who God really was. I did not know I could talk to Him the same way that I talked to my earthly father.

I knew what the preacher said, but I did not have any personal examples of where God worked things out for me specifically. In other words, I did not have that direct connection between my heavenly Father and me. I had many examples of where God worked things out with the connection of my Mom and Dad.

I was glad that I had parents that worked things out for me, but I was an adult and it would take a closer relationship with God to enable me to experience a victorious life in Jesus. It was time to activate what is stated in the Word concerning the move from milk to meat. I needed to grow-up in my walk with the Lord. I needed to demonstrate maturity and exercise my faith on a regular basis to grow through the experience of taking God at his word.

I started to notice signs of change in my thinking. I wanted to obey God and do the right thing with my life. Let's face it, if you sit under the Word and eat and drink the Word, the Word will work on you and in you.

Blinded By Love

While the Lord was working on me, the enemy was planning and plotting against me. I met a young man through one of my girlfriends and we began to date. We enjoyed each other's company but there was a problem. He had not accepted Jesus as his personal savior. Christ did not have a special meaning in his life. I knew that I enjoyed hearing the word of God, I never seemed to get enough of attending Christian events, and I really enjoyed praising God in song.

I also knew in my heart the response that the word of God has concerning unequally yoked relationships but I was enjoying myself so much that I settled for the present report over the future prediction. *"Be ye not unequally yoked together with unbelievers: for what fellowship hath righteousness with unrighteousness? and what communion hath light with darkness?"* 2 Corinthians 6:14

After a year, my life was a mess. I was involved in premarital sex, and I was asking my Savior to allow me to marry a young man that was not interested in a relationship with Christ. Clearly, I was crazy, but when you do not use the wisdom of God by consulting the Holy Spirit in your situations, you will do crazy things and think that it is God.

On one hand, I hid my non-Christ like behavior, continued to disobey God in this relationship, and on the other hand, I felt the guilt associated with disappointing God. I knew what I was doing was wrong, but I thought, if I marry him it would end the sinful part of the relationship.

Just like so many before me, I felt I could have my cake and eat it to, "if only we got married." Marriage, or so I thought, would solve all the problems at one time; a simple "I Do." I would be legal in the eyes of the law, my parents, and in the eyes of God. Last but not least, I felt if I wanted to keep him, we needed to be married (my plan, not God's).

After many months and many thoughts running through my mind, I finally decided to seek godly counsel. I met with an awesome woman of God that reminded me of a scripture that I had heard in the past. God says in his word *"Be ye not unequally yoked with unbelievers."*

This woman of God laid out my situation, applied the word of God to my situation, and sent me on my way to hopefully follow God's way. After all of her godly counsel, I chose to go against God's instruction. I felt that I was so strong in the Lord I could change my future husband into a Christian. I even found a scripture that I felt would work for me.

"For the unbelieving husband is sanctified by the wife, and the unbelieving wife is sanctified by the husband: else were your children unclean; but now are they holy." 1 Corinthians 7:14

So, I convinced myself that all was well and that all we had to do was to get married. I went against the instructions from God because I was blinded by love. God was not responding with the answers that I wanted to hear, so I went the other way. I even introduced Mom and Dad to my soon to be husband and their responses were less than supportive or positive.

My parents clearly stated, "You need to marry a person whose spiritual views are similar to yours." In my own mind, I spoke to myself and said, "They don't understand, I love him." I chose to follow my own flesh, and left with my feelings hurt but I went on with my man. Remember, I was filled with the Holy Spirit but I was not interested in Him being a part of this decision. I had not totally sold out for Christ; I was still riding the fence instead of crossing over to one side. We all deal with this fence during our Christian walk.

While flipping back and forth between the flesh and God's Word I knew the Holy Spirit was working on me because I saw changes in my behavior. My statements to my man changed drastically from let us enjoy each other, to I am afraid that Jesus will come back again while I was running around in hotels with him. I could not enjoy the sin anymore. I constantly told my future husband, "We need to get married; I can't keep living in sin." It was hard for him to enjoy me this way.

He finally gave in to my requests and I went against the instructions from God, married him, moved to another city and joined a traditional Baptist church. That was 17 years of hard marriage, but it was no one's fault but mine. I disobeyed my natural and Heavenly Father, disregarded every warning from the Holy Spirit and I reaped what I sowed.

Driven to Jesus

My marriage almost drove me crazy and almost made me lose my mind. Oh, but what the devil meant for bad, God used to drive me closer to Him to work towards my destiny. *"As for you, you meant evil against me, but God meant it for good in order to bring about this present result, to preserve many people alive." Genesis 50:20 NASB*

I began to read the Word daily and learn more about the Christian Walk. I began to want to walk, talk, think and act like Jesus did at all times. I spent my free time watching Frederick K. C. Price, T. D. Jakes, Joyce Myers, Clarence McClendon and Creflo Dollar. I watched them on television and online; I could not get enough of the Word.

As I sought to rediscover myself, I learned how to obey the Word of God, believe the Word of God, pray the Word of God, and to activate the Word of God in my life. I did not talk about the Holy Spirit that often. I discovered and used my prayer language after I was baptized in the Holy Spirit in the early 1980's, but I never used it while I was at a traditional church.

Hallelujah, my prayers were answered in 1996! I asked the Lord to send me to a church where I could get the same teaching that I received from the television ministries. The Lord led me to a non-denominational church and I enjoyed every morsel of what was taught there. I received the teaching of the Word of God in the same way I did when I was in graduate school. I grew in the wisdom and knowledge of the Lord and my life has never been the same. All the trouble during my marriage drove me to a wonderful relationship with Jesus that has gotten sweeter as the days go by. I found out that there was nobody like Jesus.

Eventually, I joined that church, and the teaching ministry was at such a level that I grew and grew in my spiritual walk. My pastor used stories and illustrations that helped me understand the word of God in a new way. I started to apply the word of God to situations in my everyday life. *God was always behind the scenes shaping my destiny.*

Conversations with the Holy Spirit

Apply The Word To Your Situations

I remember running into a couple of situations and I could hear the Holy Spirit saying to me, "apply what you've been learning in your life situations."

Pillow Sham Situation

I went to a bedding store and I bought a twin bed-in-a-bag. When I returned home, I had some extra pillow shams in my bag. I was excited that there were extra pillow shams in the bag. I had a dream of the way that I wanted that bed to look and the extra pillow shams made my dreams come true. All I could think at the time was "it's their loss, and my gain." I got what I wanted and I did not have to pay a dime.

Holy Spirit Solution

As a few days went by, every time I was alone to drive, clean my home, etc., I heard a small voice speaking to me saying, "pillow sham, pillow sham, pillow sham. Yolonda, you feel good about the two extra pillow shams on your bed but someone else is missing two pillow shams and it's because of you. Take the pillow shams back to the store so that they can handle the problem with the bed-in-the-bag that is missing the two pillow shams." Every time I heard the voice speak to me, I shook it off and kept going. My bed really looked good with those extra pillow shams in my guest bedroom.

Well, it wasn't long before the voice began to get louder and came to me more frequently. This continued until I surrendered and grabbed those two extra pillow shams and I took them back to the store. When I got to the store and found the sales person, I told her that I had bought a bed-in-the-bag and the extra two shams were in the bag. I mentioned how bad I wanted them but I knew that I needed to bring them back to the store. She looked at me and said, "You know what, you keep those two shams and enjoy yourself. You took your time and gave up your desire and brought them back." I learned a valuable lesson. When you obey the Holy Spirit, whatever it is that you desire, that is good, He will give it to you in His time. Please don't take matters into your own hands. All my life I heard that God rewards those who diligently seek him.

"Delight yourself in the LORD and he will give you the desires of your heart." Psalm 37:4

"But without faith it is impossible to please him: for he that cometh to God must believe that he is, and that he is a rewarder of them that diligently seek him." Hebrews 11:6

"You can never please God without faith, without depending on him. Anyone who wants to come to God must believe that there is a God and that he rewards those who sincerely look for him." Hebrews 11:6 TLB

When you obey him, you get blessed "BIG" time.

The Holy Spirit: The Person, The Works

Money Pouch Situation

As I continued to walk on my Christian journey, another situation reinforced my belief in the power of the Holy Spirit. I had a small pouch filled with my signed income tax check (not smart to do ahead of cashing it), a deposit slip, and a little cash. I went shopping, and came home. The next morning, as I began to dress for work, I realized that I did not have the pouch. I began to panic. I drove back to the mall, looked around in the parking lot, searched by the garbage cans, but I did not see the pouch anywhere.

I could not contact anyone in the mall because it was too early in the morning; the mall was not opened yet. So, you can probably imagine my immediate fear, that I had misplaced a signed check with hundreds of dollars for anyone to find. There was nothing I could do at the mall so, I went to work.

Holy Spirit Solution

While driving I heard the Holy Spirit say to me, "Why don't you apply all of the things that you have been learning in church.

"And in that day ye shall ask me nothing. Verily, verily, I say unto you, Whatsoever ye shall ask the Father in my name, he will give it you. Hitherto have ye asked nothing in my name: ask, and ye shall receive, that your joy may be full." John 16:23-24

"This is what I want you to do: Ask the Father for whatever is in keeping with the things I've revealed to you. Ask in my name, according to my will, and he'll most certainly give it

to you. Your joy will be a river overflowing its banks!" John 16:23-24 (MSG)

I felt confident that the Word was true and that I could ask Him for anything. I was ready to try that Word and see what the Lord would do for me. When I arrived at the office, I had pep in my step, and an air of excitement was all over me, because I had prayed and was now standing on God's Word.

I knew that God heard my prayer and I would get my pouch back. My prayer was that the Lord would give me the pouch back without a red cent or the check missing. Since I was taught to praise the Lord in advance of a blessing, I began to praise Him at that moment and did not stop until ...

Miracles Still Happen

On Monday morning I went throughout the office and told everyone in the suite, that I had lost my pouch with a big check and cash inside. I said that I believed that God would return it to me. One co-worker said "You are crazy if you think the Lord is going to give that back to you." Another co-worker stated, "Girl, whoever found your pouch will work with someone at the bank, and they will cash that check. They will probably get away with it." Immediately, my praise stopped. Once I heard their words, I began to doubt everything that I had prayed to the Lord for. I replied, "Yes you are right, I don't know why I would think that I could get that pouch back with the money in it."

Thank God that was not how the story ended because, I remembered a message that my Pastor taught on making sure that you guard your hearing and eye gates, because what you see and hear can have an effect on your faith.

Once that message was stirred up in my spirit, I saw the situation in a different way. I thought, "all I needed to do was repent, guard my eye and ear gates to stay focused on the goal, and God can change my outcome. I asked the LORD to forgive me for doubting what I had prayed. I started over again and believed that God would return the pouch. While I was waiting, I thanked God each day for bringing the pouch back with every red cent and the check in it. Every time I felt doubt began to return, I opened my mouth and praised God for doing exactly what I asked him to do and I believed that God was going to do it.

"For verily I say unto you, That whosoever shall say unto this mountain, Be thou removed, and be thou cast into the sea; and shall not doubt in his heart, but shall believe that those things which he saith shall come to pass; he shall have whatsoever he saith. Therefore I say unto you, What things soever ye desire, when ye pray, believe that ye receive them, and ye shall have them." Mark 11:23-24

Two days later, I came home from work and a message was on my answering machine stating I needed to go to the McRae's Department Store Information Desk because they have your pouch. I began to shout!!!

When I arrived at the store, the person working at the Information Desk said, "I don't have a pouch." Immediately I began to wonder if someone was playing games with me, and I returned home just a little sad.

A couple of days went by and I got a phone call from a friend that worked at the store. I asked her to check around for information concerning my lost pouch. She told me that a young lady had my pouch but she kept it in the department where she worked. The next day I went to the store and the lady was smiling when I told her my name. She had my pouch, and guess what; it had the check, and every red cent still in it, just like I asked for it in my prayer. It was a miracle!

In times like these when honest people are hard to find, there was still someone out there that God used to answer my prayer. There is really nothing too hard for God.

"Ah Lord God! behold, thou hast made the heaven and the earth by thy great power and stretched out arm, and there is nothing too hard for thee." Jeremiah 32:17

Miracles still happen. I asked the young lady if there was anything that I could do for her being so kind and she said, "Nothing at all." I told her that I made flower arrangements and wreaths. She said that she would love a wreath. So, I made her the most beautiful wreath that I ever made and she loved it. This was a great example to me of how you can take what you have been learning in church, apply it to your situation and watch God work. *God was behind the scenes shaping my destiny.*

Another Chance

"For I know the thoughts that I think toward you, saith the LORD, thoughts of peace, and not of evil, to give you an expected end." Jeremiah 29:11

I was winning in my walk with God but I was losing in my marriage. By 2002, my marriage was destroyed and I moved back to my hometown. The Holy Spirit told me that my change had only just begun. He pressed me to go back to my parent's house to start over and allow Him to take care of my children and me. I was right back where I started with my parents--but with two boys.

After I returned home, I felt like I was a failure and my life was over. I battled to overcome depression and shame with faith, and hope in all the promises that the Holy Spirit continued to say to me. *"O LORD my God, I cried unto thee, and thou hast healed me. O LORD, thou hast brought up my soul from the grave: thou hast kept me alive, that I should not go down to the pit. Psalm 30:2-3* "*God, my God, I yelled for help and you put me together. God, you pulled me out of the grave, gave me another chance at life when I was down-and-out." Psalm 30:2-3 (MSG)*

God really heard my cry, put me together and gave me another chance to walk out my God given destiny.

I remember when God saturated me with the desire to sing and write songs. In the 80's and 90's, I was writing songs and I did studio background vocals for rising songwriters. I had notebooks full of songs that I had written. I traveled with a cassette recorder and blank cassettes at all times because I wanted to be prepared to write and record the songs at any time.

I wondered why did God give me all of these songs and I never used them. Finally, a few months before I moved in with my parents, the Holy Spirit spoke to me and said it is time to use the songs that you have written and record your first CD project. So, as I headed to my hometown I did have hopes that God had something good up the road for me. God had given me another chance.

God Has Not Forgotten

After getting over the initial depression about the end of my marriage, I woke up every morning and spent my time in prayer, reading the bible, talking, and listening to God. I got instructions for my assignment for the day and I was blessed to have the time to go down that list and get to work for God. The Holy Spirit drew me back to the interdenominational church that I attended during my graduate school years and I found that they had a school of ministry. The Interdenominational School of Ministry brochure listed all of the knowledge that a student would gain from their programs. The write up mentioned minister of music and it jumped off the page and called my name. I attended the school thinking that God sent me there to prepare me to minister in music not to become a minister.

One day we had an assignment to write and deliver a message and I thought, "This has nothing to do with music." I did my assignment and as I delivered my message, the instructor gave me a weird look and said that it was good. I knew that God was birthing a music ministry in me but I had no idea that he had much more in store. *God was behind the scenes shaping my destiny.*

A Dream Come True

Singer/Songwriter/Recording Artist
God had already given me the assignment to do my first CD project before I left Vicksburg. So, I was waiting on his prompt to begin. I had been singing since I was six years old, writing songs since 1986, and now in the year of 2002, it was a dream come true when God told me, "It is time for your CD project."

My day began getting the boys ready for school. After they caught the bus every morning, I went to the dining room table to begin the work for the CD project. I had no clue of how to do or manage a CD project.

I prayed and connected with God to get instructions on how to record the project so, I prayed and God designed the CD cover. It was an awesome walk to get instructions from the Holy Spirit. He told me how the Dove, the Light, and the Cross should look on the cover. He also reminded me to ask people I had sang for over the years to sow into the project that He had for me. I prepared a sponsorship letter and sent it out to everyone that the Holy Spirit laid on my heart and people gave me over $20,000.00 for the CD Project. The Holy Spirit also sent a top gospel producer and top musicians to work with me to make the project pop with exciting music and rhythm.

The project was a Holy Spirit hook-up. I was also blessed to connect with ministries in several places throughout the nation to minister in music. The ministry time was not just singing, but I was led by the Holy Spirit to read specific scripture, testify what he led me to share from my life, and sing one song. I repeated the process with the songs that were selected for that set group of people until the Holy Spirit said end. God moved in a mighty way. I was practically on the road every weekend, but I loved it! My songs had radio play and all was well. I was so busy working, singing, and traveling I did not know my next assignment was on the way. *God was behind the scenes shaping my destiny.*

Ministering In Music - On Tour

I became business partners with my cousin, and we formed a gospel artist management company that sent Mississippi artists with anointed projects on tour throughout the nation. Our tour name was "Mississippi in the House." An unbelievable experience gave the artist a chance to spread the gospel, sell their product after each event, and enjoy using their gifts to glorify God.

We also created custom commercials, flyers, jingles, handbills for the artists and churches, conducted concerts and other events. I loved this time in my life and would have spent more time in this chapter of my life, but the Holy Spirit said, "times up" and I was called to bring the Word of God to God's people. *God was behind the scenes shaping my destiny.*

IWAPP Artist Poster   **IWAPP Event Poster**
IWAPP (International Worship & Praise Productions) a Mississippi artist company.

My Dream God's Purpose

During my time on the road ministering in music, every Monday was set aside to rest. Once the boys were on the school bus it was off to bed for me. I was so tired from the weekend events; performing the duties as Minister of Music and leading Praise and Worship at the church, I had to stop everything and sleep the entire day. While resting in bed, I heard the Holy Spirit say, "Get up, get your bible," and then He led me to John 15:16. *"Ye have not chosen me, but I have chosen you, and ordained you, that ye should go and bring forth fruit, and that your fruit should remain: that whatsoever ye shall ask of the Father in my name, he may give it you."*

I read this scripture, wondered what it was talking about and then I began my research. The Holy Spirit soon revealed the message that He had for me. He explained, *"I called you, or I picked you, to work for me. I ordained you, designated you, set you apart for my work. This was a divine setup. Whom I ordain, I qualify so that their work of spreading the gospel will be successful. Affect the world wherever I place you and make a difference that lasts into the future. Focus on doing what I want to do through your life."*

Well, God had spoken and I laid in bed meditating on His message. I remembered that many people told me that I preached during my concerts. I always responded with these words, "God did not tell me anything about preaching. I don't see that at all." I shall never forget the Monday that He took me to that scripture and reminded me of situations that confirmed that He called me to Work for Him. I was living out my dream and He called me to work in his purpose.

Wow, God called me to preach. Yolonda, a sorority girl past who never missed a party. The girl who entered so many dance contests, they called me "Miss Social Girl" – yes, God called me to work for Him.

I told my mother about my talk with the Holy Spirit and she said, "God has called you, girl." I went to my pastor and shared everything and he said, "What took you so long to tell me?" Once I released the call from God, He began to move all the pieces to fit in the puzzle of my life.

My God is strategic. He had me in school, traveling the country ministering in music, licensed and ready to preach and operating in the positions within my church. He had it all planned. I was living my dream and working in God's purpose. What a mighty God we serve. *God was behind the scenes shaping my destiny.*

Now Go To Work

Assignment #1 - Ministering On the Road

I began receiving invitations, not just to sing but also to preach. God was using me in a mighty way and I could not thank Him enough. I continued to tell Him, "I love what You are doing with my life. My Dream and Your Purpose is a Holy Spirit Hook-Up."

After several years, the invitations on the road became slim, and I found myself having more and more work at my local church. It is time for my next assignment. I was not ready to switch assignments but I learned to flow with the move of the Holy Spirit. As my former pastor in Jackson, Mississippi said, "You better get under the spout where the Glory is coming out." *God was behind the scenes shaping my destiny.*

Assignment #2 - Ministering In My Local Church

God made me available to assist the pastor with many of the tasks needed in the church because I did not have a job at the time. The Lord kept His word that He would take care of my children and me. We did not lose anything during the time that I did not have a regular job, because God supernaturally sent the money in from the work that He sent me to do. Our church was a new ministry that started out of my childhood church and I was the first minister that my pastor licensed in that facility. Our church was not a mega church. We had a small congregation and there was much work to do with limited resources. I was not on the payroll but God took care of my family like royalty.

The Holy Spirit allowed me to start, what turned out to be a wonderful prayer ministry. We created a prayer box for the congregation to place their requests to God and we met once a week to study a book on effective prayer. We also prayed over the requests. Soon, I began to lead the women of the church to have a fundraiser to assist in funds for a church trip. We had a "Hat Affair" fundraiser that featured beautiful hats and fashions from around the country.

I was in my element and moving with the guidance of the Holy Spirit. I also became the minister of music at the church. This assignment was a lot of work so God sent a few musically blessed people to assist me. We gathered the music and prepared the three-part harmony for every funeral, every special program, praise and worship and choir songs for Sunday service. That assignment was fun, because I loved music and I had worked in the music arena for so many years, but this was more than the work done in the studio and there was not a button to push to redo a mess up.

One of the best assignments during my time in my home church was getting the opportunity to preach, and I preached anytime that my pastor needed me. He was not selfish about sharing the pulpit on Sunday, and he called on me many times. *God was behind the scenes shaping my destiny.*

Assignment #3 - Ministered In My Community
There was never a dull moment during my time in Columbus because the Holy Spirit kept me productive and

at work. For my next assignment, the Holy Spirit instructed me to have containers of blessed oil in my vehicle, just in case someone needed prayer and I could act immediately on His instructions. It was wonderful, but a challenge to be used by God to make a difference in someone's life. God did not always assign me to people that I knew, or people that looked or sounded appealing, but the outcome was always great. I knew that God was with me and I was glad to be in His army. I thank God for the training ground that was tailor made just for me. I had no idea that another assignment was on the way. *God was behind the scenes shaping my destiny.*

Assignment #4 - The Holy Spirit Research

One day in 2005, the Sunday School teacher discussed the lesson concerning the Holy Spirit. The adult class members discussed their views on the subject and there was a little disagreement in their responses. The pastor was in another location in the church, and not available to clear up the matter. Internally, I said, "Why won't someone here handle this problem?"

The Holy Spirit said, "*You handle it. Go research on this topic like never before. Let me explain this to you so that you can help the traditional churches that don't spend much time discussing the Holy Spirit.*"

Every time my children went to visit their dad, I got depressed. The Holy Spirit flipped the script on me and told me to utilize that time to study and gather the information as instructed. In 2007, I began teaching on the subject as the Holy Spirit opened doors, and also offered a pamphlet for a small donation. *God was behind the scenes shaping my destiny.*

Assignment #5 - Ministering at the YMCA

Around 2008, the Lord sent me on my next assignment to volunteer in the Prison ministry at the YMCA. I was able to present God's word once a month and watched God create giants for His work through the women affected by incarcerated loved ones. These women went through tough times but they did not allow the tough times to keep them down. Each month we were encouraged to stay connected to God and allow the Holy Spirit to teach us how to obtain God's purpose for our life, no matter what we had to endure.

A couple of times a year all the women went on a retreat and we served and ministered to these women. I had never met the needs of people like this before. This was not only life changing for the women but it changed me. After the retreat, I felt as if I had been in the trenches working with God's people to accomplish God's purpose. I realized that I had experienced what I called trench ministry. Most of my assignments in the past were platform ministry. You preached, sang, or taught on a stage or platform and brought a mighty Word from God, believed that the Word changed lives, expected results and went home when the work was complete. This is great work, but I had not experienced the other side of ministry before that assignment. God started to develop love in my heart for his people. Little did I know that this assignment would lead to a full-time job as Assistant Director of Christian Emphasis and Teen Director at the YMCA. This was the first time I received a salary to do the work of God.

I spent two glorious years at the YMCA and I met some of the most wonderful people in the world. This was an example of trench ministry at its best. While there, I worked with a lady that was a living example of *service* and *submission* to the Lord. We prayed before every event, we prayed before every meeting, we prayed for God to send the workers, and show us the proper way to operate. Then, we witnessed Him work. Volunteers came from the north, south, east and west! What a miracle! We created a ministry room, prayed for God to send furniture and He answered our prayer.

Later, we facilitated "Lunch & Learn" for women to study the bible. Some of the lessons featured biblical videos and it was just an hour of power, where lives were transformed. We had six-week classes where we studied from books that were life changing for men and women.

As Y-Teen Director, I taught "Life Skills" to teen's 9th-12th grade, in four high schools. The Holy Spirit designed the classes to prepare high school seniors for life after graduation. They received education on personal finance, higher education, dating, and career opportunities.

We also offered "Knocking It Off." The book we used to conduct the classes was entitled "Journey To Healthy Living." We taught teens how to knock off the tricks of the enemy such as: unwanted weight, depression, anorexia, bulimia, or negative thoughts that were not of God in order to become all God created them to be. We taught them to operate in his purpose concerning their life. The study and exercise classes covered a six-week period, and we were challenged physically and mentally. The structure was divided into group discussions and total body workouts.

We also facilitated ACT Prep which prepared teens to perform better on the standardized tests. It was a blessing to see the student scores increase as a result of this prep class. Teens were transformed through the Teen Program and other organizations collaborated with us to help fight world hunger. Some other programs we executed were: STOP HUNGER NOW-teens packed dried food to feed families in third world countries. EMPTY BOWLS-teens made and sold ceramic bowls to send the funds to Africa for an orphanage.

We ended the year with a trip to a camp in the Carolina Mountains that took us on a spiritual purpose-driven adventure. The world as we knew it stopped and we experienced a week full of activities that created an encounter with God that was closer than we ever had before. We came home ready to move forward with Jesus. I had so much fun and grew in the Lord during this assignment. Our lives were never the same.

God also used me as the liaison between the YMCA and an elementary school. The school was near the YMCA so the kids walked over to receive teaching in basic exercise and character building. I also taught character building for a middle school once a week. The job that God called me to do at the YMCA was a mighty work and it changed my life. *God was behind the scenes shaping my destiny.*

Assignment #6 - Ministering Through Service Learning
The YMCA position opened the door for other jobs. God was not through with me yet. He used me to work

in an after school program that allowed me to teach one of my favorite things since I had come back home, service learning. Teaching youth to serve their community for a lifetime and not just volunteer for a season was awesome. I prayed and the Holy Spirit developed a curriculum for the service learning class and equipped me to teach it to middle school students during the year and the summer. The class was designed to take a field trip every week to activate what we learned by working in an organization.

At Operation Uganda, we sorted and packed clothes, wheel chairs, and walkers. We washed five-gallon buckets to send to Africa for carrying water and market shopping supplies. The middle school students saw life from a servant's view instead of a "serve me" view. It was amazing to see how it changed them.

I was in my hometown paper often shining for Jesus. Everything that was done through my mortal body was only accomplished by the move of the Holy Spirit. I can do nothing without God and I soon experienced how to operate as a servant leader. *God was behind the scenes shaping my destiny.*

A Holy Spirit Hook Up

Clearly, I had prayed and reaped the benefit of the Holy Spirit's guidance but did not think to watch out for the enemy. The enemy was not happy with me and he began to spin a web. He knows how to trap us. If he cannot attract you with sex, drugs, or money, he will find your weak spot. I was so busy working for the Lord that I was not taking care of myself. I had a problem. I loved to work and do great things for the Lord so much that I would not say no when I was faced with too many requests.

God's Work during My Stay in Columbus
- 2003-released a Gospel CD Project
- 2003 - ISM Graduate
- 2004-2010 Minister of Music/Praise & Worship Leader
- 2004-Co-Founder of IWAPP
- A Mississippi Artist Company
- 2005-licened as a Minister
- 2006-wrote songs and recorded with other artists
- 2005-2010 Minister in my church
- 2007-wrote The Person & Work of the Holy Spirit Pamphlet
- 2008-Assistant Director of Christian Emphasis Department & Teen Director -YMCA
- 2010-Licened & Ordained as an Elder

My children and I stayed home with my parents from 2002-2010. *God was behind the scenes shaping my destiny.*

My workload increased and my private time with God decreased. I was only able to do all of these assignments by the grace and protection of God. I was so stretched thin that I was about to pop.

"Watch and pray, that you enter not into temptation: the spirit indeed is willing but the flesh is weak." Matthew 26:41

He reminded me that He had lots of work for me to do but if I overload myself, I wouldn't be here to do the work. He told me that I was helping the devil out. I began to cry and feel tired and overwhelmed because I felt like I never had enough time to do what I needed to do. There were days that I had to pray my way through the entire day to make it back home that night. The Holy Spirit heard my cry and dealt with me about not saying no to any request. It was a problem! So, he sent my Boaz, just in time to catapult me into my next assignment. Won't God Do It?

God had prepared a soul mate for me in the midst of all of the assignments and challenges. We grew up together as children and came from the same spiritual background. I experienced Holy dating - no sex before marriage, or God's way of dating. When you date God's way, the report from the devil will read: will not work, will not get you a spouse, and will leave you lonely. The devil is a liar.

I dated my husband God's way from 2004-2010. At first, we really did not date. We talked on the phone a lot and saw each other twice a month to go to the movies, eat out, or we spent time with each other's families since our families were friends since we were kids. He treated me like a queen. This was a courtship from heaven or my favorite saying: a Holy Spirit Hookup.

I still had battles: a son in college, a son in elementary school both without their Dad but the wonderful things that were happening to us were worth the decision to live God's way. I knew that the Holy Spirit was with me; leading me, protecting me, providing for me, teaching me, telling me things to come, and bringing things to my remembrance, etc. This was supernatural. I knew God the Father who created me, I knew God the Son who saved me, and now I know God the Holy Spirit. What a Walk!

New Beginnings

In 2009, seven years had passed after I left Vicksburg, MS. In the bible, seven is the number of completion; God had done some things in me that prepared me for my next assignment.

In 2010, eight years had passed. In the bible, eight is the number of new beginnings. I was about to start the new beginning that God set up for me. I finally re-married on Sept 4, 2010, and by the power of the Holy Spirit, we were sex-free until our wedding night. What a mighty God we serve. God blessed me for being faithful to continue to work for Him. God told me that the wedding would be an encouragement to women to not settle for Ishmael but hold out for your Isaac, the blessing from God for you.

Donell and I worked so well together; loving and obeying God, family, and others. We moved to Atlanta and the next phase of my life began. The first year all I did was spend time with God, unpack, position things in our home, take care of my younger son, enjoy my husband, and check on my parents and my older son who were all still in Mississippi. This was a resting period for me. I did not write many songs and I was not working nor had we joined a church.

In 2011, we joined Changing a Generation (CAG) Full Gospel Baptist Church and it was not long before I began to work. I was informed about the three-ministry work limit to keep people balanced. So, I followed that rule and I sang in the choir, became a member of the College of Elders, and I helped with the youth ministry. The second year the Holy Spirit led me to work with Lead

Empowerment instead of the youth ministry and volunteer at the charter school where my younger son attended.

The old problem started to resurface. People began to contact me from Mississippi, Georgia, Chicago, etc. for ministry work (singing, teaching, and preaching). I became full-time at the charter school, and my workload increased. To top it all off, my parents became ill and moved in with us.

My parents were hospitalized eight times, over three years, between the two of them, and I was telling everyone yes again. I ended up in bed for a couple of months with shingles. I was flat on my back crying to God and He told me, "*You have been in this place before Yolonda. You are trying to be all things to all people and that is My job. You work and work and you do not get enough rest. You must take care of yourself so that you can have a long productive life working for me. Your assignment is over at the school. I sent you to help and you "ran out," or went overboard with all that you volunteered to do. Before that assignment ended at the middle school, you trained all of the soloists in the after school performing arts program, you were the activity director, the counselor, the substitute teacher assistant, the testing coordinator, and more. You had duties at the church, taking care of your parents, raising a middle school student, and taking care of home because your husband works away from home. What a web you made.*"

I was so overwhelmed it was worse than before. I added more and more things and never dropped anything. The Holy Spirit supped with me as I lay in the bed for a couple of months. *God was behind the scenes shaping my destiny.*

Sweet Communion

First, I repented for not getting permission from my heavenly father for everything that I did and getting so BUSY.

Being
Under
Satan's
Yolk

We become busy when we allow satan to overload us beyond our God instructed limitations and rob us of our freedom to operate in our destiny.

The enemy is walking around seeking whom he may devour in whatever area that he can. If he cannot trick you to become a whoremonger, drug addict, thief, alcoholic, abuser, liar, atheist, or lover of power, he will get some of us off track by using the BUSY trick.

We are so excited to be used by God, that we forget that we are human and it is all about Him. We need to follow the Holy Spirit's lead to His purpose for our life and let us strive for no more and certainly no less than what He instructs. God knows what is best for us, so stay in His perfect will.

Once I repented, the Lord shared some of the assignments that He had for me. He had such sweet communion with me in that bed. The talks He had with me were priceless; He healed me and released me for several assignments. I invited the Holy Spirit to talk to me all day long. I need Him, I cannot and do not want to live without Him. Activating the work of the Holy Spirit, or my

Holy Spirit hook-up, in my daily life is necessary for every believer.

The Holy Spirit said, "A*dd another chapter to the Holy Spirit pamphlet, begin the jingle business that I created you to do, start your next recording project, and continue allowing me to use you in the Word and music ministry to build My kingdom."*

It was such a blessing to commune with the Holy Spirit and get instructions for my next assignment. I loved spending time with the Holy Spirit! After a couple of months, I regained my strength and began the next phase of my life. *God was behind the scenes shaping my destiny.*

Past Experiences Teach Valuable Lessons

When I was dating my first husband, I prayed to God to see if He wanted me to continue to date him or let him go. God's instructions were to let him go, but I continued to date him. Later on in the relationship, when it was time to marry him the Lord told me to let him go because we were unequally yoked.

Again, I followed my own directions and married him. This was 17 years of a very rough marriage all because I did not follow the instructions that the Holy Spirit gave me. Now, I found myself married again in a marriage that was totally ordained by God. What a difference between being married from your own hook up and being married from a Holy Spirit hook up. I know now that my ex-husband was OK especially since he has accepted Christ in his life and I was OK, we just were not OK together.

When the marriage is a hook up of yours the arguments, the fights, the disagreements, the trouble, and the struggle is so hard and so rough. When the marriage is a Holy Spirit hook up, through the arguments, troubles, struggles, and issues we always get the victory because our relationship is rooted and grounded in the Lord and we allow the Holy Spirit to lead us, cover and protect us. This is an awesome walk in Holy Matrimony.

To live with the one that God kept for me is fabulous. To see the evidence of God's promises concerning me filled my heart with Joy, and made me want to run and tell everybody that *God Is Real*. I continue to get proof that the Word is true and the Holy Spirit has a job concerning me. I am determined to allow the Holy Spirit to work on my behalf and live the life that God has planned for me. I do not want to live without the Holy Spirit ruling and abiding in me. Holy Spirit you can have your way with me.

Chapter 5

Moving Forward To My Destiny

My husband and I started our business, Smith-II-Smith Enterprises Inc. in 2013, and our mission is to help families and small businesses achieve financial goals through financial education, jingles, and graphics.

The task we faced seemed impossible to accomplish, along with all of our other roles, without the Holy Spirit. God blessed my husband with a Master's Degree in Finance and International Business and the wisdom, knowledge and understanding in the financial world. His gift is to make "your money" make more money for you.

God gave me the gift of creativity and imagination to write, arrange, and sing jingles. My gift allows a simple tune, song and music sell your business. He and I took the opportunity to activate the mission of our business through the lives of people. It's a great feeling to work with the love of your life for the God who loves us greater than anyone else. God made us and put us together for his purpose and we were excited as we move forward to our destiny.

When you decide to operate in your God given purpose, the devil has set himself to kill, steal, and destroy every good thing that God has set up for you (John 10:10). I had to remember the scripture concerning the devil walking about seeking who he can devour with his tricks and traps (1 Peter 5:8).

I was enjoying life so much that when God gave me my assignment, I wanted to go quickly and get it done with excellence. I forgot that some assignments are long term and take discipline and time to accomplish.

Discipline means to follow the new plan God gave me although my day-to-day tasks have become increasingly more demanding.

The Lord told me to leave my job, be a wife, be a mother, become a caregiver for my Mom (78) and Dad (81), write this book, start a jingle business, record my next music project, and work in the church.

My family and church roles took on a life of their own and I completed very little on the other assignments God gave me. I was glad I was doing these tasks but I did not please God when I moved so slowly on the book and the jingles. In my spirit, I heard God say *"You are helping the devil out and destroying your destiny when you don't handle everything my way and in my time."*

The devil tried to mess up God's plan anyway he could. The enemy stole a part of my blessing because I did something a little late. I had to make sure I took every situation to God in prayer, as I love to do, and continue to mature by obeying God's instructions to the letter. Although my plate was full, I began to pay more attention to the details.

The Details

I. *Praying*: Talking to God.
II. *Meditation*: Being quiet, waiting to hear God's answers and instructions.
III. *Obey*: Doing exactly what God says.

It took a lot of discipline to make a schedule and a lot of energy to follow it. I ran to do everything for everyone else and when I was done, I crawled into bed and passed out. I never made time to work on the book.

I soon realized the way I had handled my normal day had to change. I was caring for my parents, raising my 15-year-old, being a wife, counseling my 25-year-old, and ministering through singing and preaching the Word. All of these hats took so much of my time that I found myself desperately wanting to finish this book and longing to get back in the studio to write and record songs and jingles.

I felt down because I could not get all of my God-given assignments done. Day after day, something happened that I could not change or put off until later; duty to the family called me away or another fire had to be put out. After the emergency passed, I was so tired that I was not in a work or book writing mood. I did not get my work done. I could not believe I had allowed the devil to keep me in his demonic trap for over two years. I had heard stories concerning people losing years and never finishing a project. I could not believe it had happened to me; the workaholic, the get-it-done girl, the hard working reliable sister, or 'Miss *Speedy*'.

God had not educated me, empowered me, equipped me, anointed me, and appointed me, to go down like that. I realized the enemy was winning unless I changed or shifted my priorities. I had to believe that I was an *overcomer* by the blood of the lamb and the word of my testimony. I activated the Holy Spirit to help me, guide me, protect me and elevate me to the next level. I rose early in the morning, prayed in the natural, prayed in the spirit, read the word, spent time with the Lord and allowed Him minister to me.

I poured out to Him and He responded. I told Him that I could not handle all the things that had been thrust upon me and I needed His Holy Spirit to rescue me from not only myself, but also the situation. I cried out, *"Lord, I can't do what you have asked me to do on my own, I need you NOW!"*

When I spent my time with Him, I experienced what I call, "His Flip the Script Method." If I was sick, I walked out healed. If I felt burdened, I walked out free because I put the burden in God's hands. I gave God everything through my song, my prayer, my cry, and my dance. My special area for this was the sitting area in my bedroom and I did not move until He talked to me.

When I was done, I was all right and God answered my call by giving me my daily tasks. I pushed hard each day to accomplish exactly what He said. In order to soar I had to obey His voice, and today my life is where God wants it to be.

I followed the schedule that the Holy Spirit gave me and now I enjoy the blessed life. It is a daily challenge to follow this process. The book is now complete, jingles have been written and produced and I am planning my next CD project, accepting more preaching and singing assignments. God showed up once again: Won't He Work Everything Out?

Chapter 6

The Holy Spirit Blueprint

blueprint to follow to allow the Holy Spirit to lead you daily so that you never live without Him.

Go To Your Prayer Spot - find your favorite quite space in your home.

Invite the Holy Spirit - to have his way and become the ruler of your life. A Sample Prayer:

> Father in the name of Jesus,
> Be my guest. I invite you Holy Spirit to fill me, to take control of my life and perform every work that God the Father has ordained and predestined for me. Have your way with me. Into your hands, I lay every gift, every dream, and all my trust in you. Take control of me and lead me today. I declare and decree that I operate with the mind of Christ and the wisdom, knowledge, and understanding of God. Cover me with the blood of Jesus. No weapon formed against me and my house shall prosper. Instruct and teach me the way that you would have me to go and guide me with your eyes. I will walk in my Destiny, Make it to my Destination, and Operate in the Purpose God has for me. So God Shape My Destiny.
>
> In Jesus name I pray,
> Amen

Pray in the spirit to allow the Holy Spirit to control your tongue and let go.

Pray in the natural. Use the Lord's Prayer and make it personal. Thank God for all that he has done and will do. Tell God all of your issues, concerns, problems, etc.

Read the Word and use a daily devotional and study the scriptures. Get a "Read the Bible in a Year" reading plan. You can find these on the internet or at your local Christian Book Store.

Meditate by spending time with the Lord. Play soft worship music to set the atmosphere.

One of my favorite worship songs is Larnell Harris, "*I Miss My Time With You.*" The words to this song is:

> There He was just waiting
> In our old familiar place
> An empty spot beside Him
> Where once I used to wait
> To be filled with strength and wisdom
> For the battles of the day
> I would've passed Him by again
> But I clearly heard Him say
> I miss my time with you
>
> Those moments together
> I need to be with you each day
> And it hurts me when you say
> You're too busy, busy trying to serve Me
> But how can you serve Me
> When your spirit's empty
> There's a longing in My heart
> Wanting more than just a part of you
> It's true

I miss My time with you

What will I have to offer
How can I truly care
My efforts have no meaning
When your presence isn't there
But You'll provide the power
If I take time to pray
I'll stay right here beside You
And you'll never have to say

Sit quite in your spot tell the Holy Spirit that I am reporting for duty and let the Holy Spirit minister to you.

Journal what the Holy Spirit says to you.

Obey the commands from the Holy Spirit throughout your day.

Watch God work for you and enjoy the blessed life.

The effects of entering the Lord's presence;

- If you enter in prayer wounded, you can come out a warrior.
- If you enter a victim, you can come out a victor.
- If you enter sick, you can come out healed
- If you enter discouraged, you can come out encouraged.
- If you enter a mess, you can come out with a miracle.

The Holy Spirit is our helper; He fixed things for me and He will fix things for you. The Holy Spirit, the person, the works, don't live without Him!

Christian Walk

The graph displays that the only way to reach 100% of the purpose God plans for you, is the ability to grow from just being saved to walking in the power of the Holy Spirit.

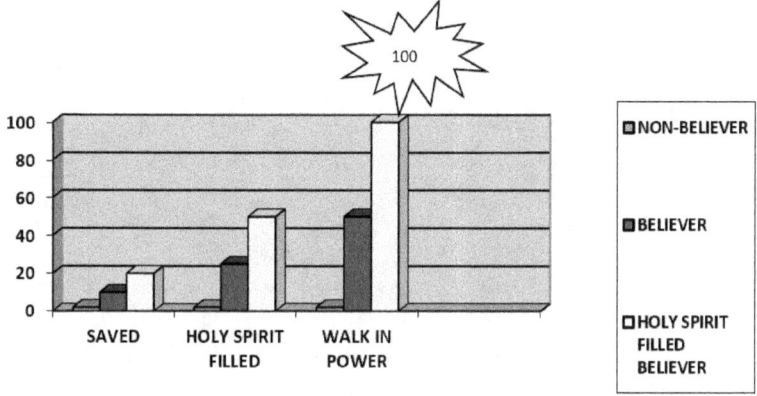

Steps to a Blessed Life

- *Non-Believer* - A person who has not accepted Jesus as their personal savior.
- *Saved* - Sinner accepted Jesus as their personal savoir, and Holy Spirit takes up residence.
- *Holy Spirit Filled* - Believer filled with the Holy Spirit (evidence) and has surrendered all to God.
- *Walk in Power* - Believer has and will continue to overcome the demonic traps and attacks and takes dominion over all areas of life until you go to be with the Lord.

PO Box 453
Powder Springs, GA 30127
770-727-6517

info@entegritypublishing.com

www.info@entegritypublishing.com

www.ingramcontent.com/pod-product-compliance
Lightning Source LLC
Chambersburg PA
CBHW070544300426
44113CB00011B/1786